# THE COWBOY

*A CONTEMPORARY PHOTOGRAPHIC STUDY*
*BY ROBERT REYNOLDS*

International Standard Book Number 0-912856-20-3
Library of Congress Catalog Number 75-1651
Copyright© 1975 by Graphic Arts Center Publishing Co.
2000 N.W. Wilson • Portland, Oregon 97209 • 503/224-7777
Designer • Robert Reynolds
Printer • Graphic Arts Center
Bindery • Lincoln & Allen
Printed in the United States of America

"I wouldn't want to live in town. Some o' them ol' boys, hell—they don't even know a good bean feed."

"You can almost tell a genuine cowboy by his riding gear . . . I've been on spreads where they'd look at your gear b'fore they'd ask you any questions."

''Slow an' deliberate. That's the way to rope horses. That way ya' won't rile 'em up.''

"Shoein's tricky business. Cut a foot too short or quick a horse—that's a good way to be left afoot nine miles from home."

"Ridin' and ropin's o.k., but I'd sooner have a good cup a' coffee—or a woman."

"I've seen superintendents and I've seen superintendents. Some of them can do everything, and know everything that's goin' on. But some of them have to ask which end of the cow is grazin'."

"Lot'a things ya' can say about a cowboy and most of 'em would be true. But it's got to be about cattle. That's the name of the game. No cows—no cowboys."

"Why, when I'm workin' a cow with that ol' grey cuttin' horse, I'm just a passenger."

"In the old days, if a man couldn't ride, he'd better not go to these ranches. Used to have to be a cowboy. You don't have to be a cowboy on some of them anymore, though it sure helps."

"The elements are what we're always up against—cold, ice and snow. Or maybe dry and dusty and no rain. But we all knew that when we signed on!"

"There's a whole lot'a bluff to a bull, and a whole lot that ain't."

"The cook's still boss around his wagon. I've seen 'em where he'd take a stick and draw off a place around the wagon, and you better not do anything inside that line unless you ask him about it."

"I've heard ol' boys make little of the wrangler, but to me, well, he's really important. You need someone to take good care of your horses.

"I've seen 'em move a remuda and have horses so give out you wouldn't want to ride 'em. A good wrangler will just grass his horses across country and kind of time it so's that when he gets there, the horses are in good shape."

"Man's got to watch a horse's ears. That's the indicator. And you feel him tightnin' up lotsa' times, before he goes to pitchin' or do anything."

"I worked for outfits that if they catch ya' fightin a horse—well, ya' just better go draw your pay."

"Gimme a good dog and I can do the work of three men. Hell, ya' go out after a calf and he might run a mile. Dog'll just go out there and bite him on the nose, and he'll run ya' down gettin' back into the herd. And you haven't left your station to boot. But a dog's gotta learn to stay back, too."

"The ideal place to brand is right there in the pasture. Then when you're through they'll get together and mother up."

"The pickup truck and trailer has revolutionized cowboyin'.

Ya' don't need as many horses any more, an' instead of ridin' to the back side of the pasture they haul 'em in a trailer.

" 'Course the truck revolutionized rustlin', too. More goin' on today than ever before."

''Workin' the pens is a hot, dirty job. Sometimes a cow might git it in her head to just run right over a man.''

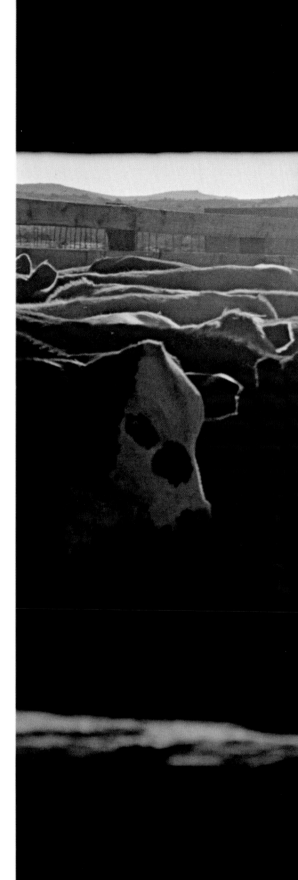

"Ya' betcha' squeeze chutes are important. Maybe it's 'cause they ain't so many good cowboys around, and rancher's still gotta brand."

"Heifer calves, they cut the ear marks, an' save 'em. On bull calves, they save the tip they cut off the bag. That way you keep a tally.

"But a tally's more interesting when you have the help of a purty girl to count for you."

"Used to be a man with a maverick ring, a good rope and a good horse could start up a herd purty soon. Kind of frowned on by the best people, though."

"Done a whole lotta flankin' in my life, and at one time thought I was about as good as the next man, 'cause I had so much practice."

"One man gets the rope, the other the tail. Don't jerk too hard, just enough to get 'em down. Two men who work together can make it twice as easy—and easier on the stock."

"Sandy, why ya' got just one spur on?"

"I only need one. I figure if I can get one side to goin' the other'll keep up. Course I may go in a big arc."

"Best way to train a horse is to start when he's young, and get him to likin' ya'. Get a horse not to be afraid, you can handle him. A horse afraid of me, I'm afraid of him.

"Where there's fear there's hate— where there's hate, there's danger. A horse that's been mistreated, ya' better watch him. He may forget sometime."

''A horse throwed this ol' boy off. He climbed up out of the dust, an' he said, 'If that's all ya' got for me to ride, I quit.' The foreman rode by, an' he said, 'Hell, we got a hundred, but they's all just like him.' ''

"To make a cow horse out'a them, ya' git 'em used to everything. Throw a lot'a ropes over 'em and git 'em used to the slicker. Horse is only afraid of what he doesn't understand."

"Weather don't mean a thing. If it's rainin', you just put your slicker on. If it's purty out leave it to home. One time I was out lookin' for cattle, weather was so bad I was wishin' I wouldn't find 'em."

"This here's big country. It's so quiet you can hear daylight coming."

"Ya' can't teach a horse so much haulin' 'em around as you can ridin' 'em. An' he can't teach you as much, either."

"Whether a rancher dies rich or poor really depends on what the cattle market was the day before."